CITY OF SAFARI

by
Helen Long

photographs by
Edith Wynne-Williams

ABSON BOOKS · ABSON · WICK · BRISTOL

*For my children, Christopher, Rosemary, David
and Timothy who enjoyed animal hunting with me.*

First published in Great Britain in 1983
by ABSON BOOKS, Abson, Wick, Bristol.

Set in Baskerville 11 on 12 pt

ISBN 0 902920 52 9

Printed at the Burleigh Press, Bristol, England

Dragon marking an entrance to the square mile of the City. (See page 25.)

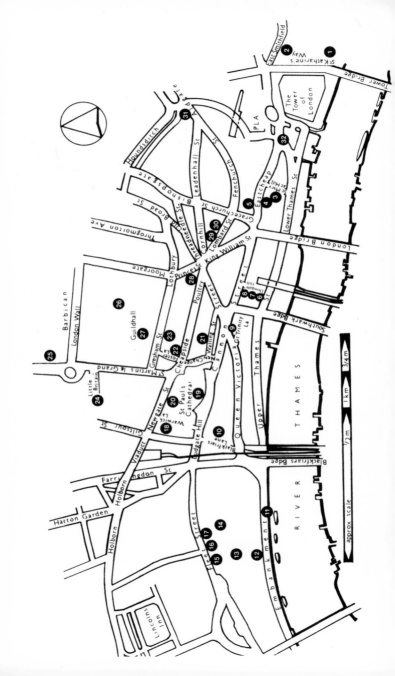

CONTENTS

INTRODUCTION

I know a charming lion who lives at St. Paul's Cathedral. But he is just one of the many creatures who, over the generations, have taken up residence in the City of London, the most valuable square mile anywhere in the world.

Some of these animals, birds, insects, and reptiles live modestly at less prestigious addresses, usually well hidden in their secret lairs, and always with a very good and historically interesting reason for being where they are.

City of London Safari will help you to find them. And they are all to be seen free by anyone who knows where to go in search of them.

As you walk around London's City you will find yourself visiting new, and often less well-known places, and becoming familiar with some of the smaller churches built by Sir Christopher Wren, as well as with his great masterpiece St. Paul's Cathedral.

Some of these creatures will be more easily spotted than others for some are worn with age, ravaged by the weather, by the Great Fire of 1666, or by the high explosive and incendiary bombs of World War II. But all are worth tracking down and getting to know.

City of London Safari will incline you to look up – and down – and perhaps thereafter to look at buildings and statues with a new and seeing eye.

HELEN LONG

GIRL WITH A DOLPHIN

St. Katharine's Way, beside Tower Hotel, below Tower Bridge

A small girl plays with a dolphin in a shower of spray. The work of David Wynne, in 1973.

Ivory House, The World Trade Centre, St. Katharine's Docks

Two elephants guard the entrance to the vast new development, covering the 27 acre site of the Old St. Katharine's Docks.

In this complex, some of the existing historic and commercial buildings have been restored, and adapted to new uses, whilst continuing to give character and atmosphere to the whole enterprise.

The Ivory House, which is now transformed into luxury residential apartments, was built between 1856 and 1880 as a warehouse to contain precious imported ivory from Africa and India.

This beautiful and secure building was at one time the centre of the ivory trade in London and handled the raw material which was to become ever more popular and in demand.

For the early Victorian period saw an increasing use of ivory for thousands of piano keys, for decoration and inlay in elegant furniture, as escutcheons and trinkets, for chess-men, counters, gambling games, hair-brushes and combs, napkin rings, and jewellery.

Much of this ivory also found it way to the Cutlers, to be used as handles for the quality knives so beloved of the Victorians, to match their fine table silver, and to denote prosperity and good taste.

Elephants therefore loom large here, where the ivory was unloaded from great ships, and stored in the Ivory House: as they do at the Cutlers' Hall in Warwick Lane.

The two elephants on the gate pillars were placed there by the property developers, St. Katharine-by-the-Tower Ltd, as a permanent reminder of the importance of this building, and the docks here, and of the pattern of life at the turn of the century.

DOLPHINS

Watermen's Hall, St. Mary at Hill

The Company of Watermen and Lightermen on the river Thames can trace its history right back to the time of the construction of the first stone bridge across the Thames in London (1186–1209).

From the earliest times this great river has been a main highway for those living and working in London.

In 1514 Parliament had found it necessary to introduce some form of control over the many thousands who earned a living on or about the river: and this Act regulated fares to be charged.

In 1598 a survey of London claimed that forty thousand men earned a living in some fashion connected with the river, some of them having served an apprenticeship for a year to learn the Waterman's trade: a period which was later extended to seven years under an Act of 1603.

In 1700 the Lightermen, who hitherto had been members of the Woodmongers' Company, succeeded in their petitions to Parliament, and the Act of that year brought them into the Watermens' Company.

From then on Lightermen were bound by the same regulations as applied to Watermen, and in succeeding years their numbers grew with the ever-increasing trade of the Port of London, while those of the Watermen diminished, due to the improvement of road transport in the Cities of London and Westminster.

Here, a pair of Dolphins frolic on either side of a shield on which a boat is seen floating on the river, and above it a pair of crossed oars are flanked by a couple of cabin cushions.

Peek House
20 Eastcheap

The business premises of Peek Winch and Todd, importers of eastern spices and other goods.

This firm did much business with the Grocers' Company, which also dealt in spices, as their coat of arms with its nine cloves depicts.

The camel, too, surmounts the Grocers' armorial bearings, laden with goods from the Far East, as are these three camels who carry theirs around the corner of the building into Eastcheap.

TWO MICE EATING SANDWICHES
23–25 Eastcheap, Philpot Lane

Whilst craftsmen were busily working on this elaborately decorated nineteenth century building, they were plagued with mice, and daily watched the greedy and brazen little creatures tucking into the sandwiches they brought with them to work.

To commemorate these daring mice who had become such an integral part of their day's work, they left behind them when their job was completed this affectionate little carving for the pleasure of posterity.

THE SPOTTED LEOPARDS OF
THE MISTERY OF DYERS

Dowgate Hill

The Dyers were first mentioned as a guild in 1188, and powers of self-regulation were granted to the Dyers Craftsmen in 1310–1311.

The Dyers Company in the past was the twelfth of the Great City Livery Companies, following in all proceedings and standings, next after the Vintners: then, as now, the eleventh Company.

But in January 1516 it was adjudicated that "the Wardens and Fellowship of the Dyers shall charitably and lovingly follow next the Wardens and Fellowship of Shearmen (now represented by the Cloth workers), in all processions, goings, standings, and ridings, without any further strife or debate," thus becoming, as they still are, the thirteenth Company.

> *"An Haberdasher and a Carpenter,*
> *A Webbe, a Dyer, and a Tapiser*
> *Clothed in oo liveree*
> *Of a solemn and great fraternitiee."*

These lines of about 1390 are from the *Canterbury Tales* of Geoffrey Chaucer, himself a member of the Vintner's Company, with which the Dyers have old associations in keeping the swans on the Thames.

This privilege of the Dyers of having a Royalty of a game of swans on the Thames is said to go back to before 1483. The cygnets are taken up each July for indentification, and to witness this, the Wardens attend for a day, the annual Swan Upping Voyage.

Identification is now by one mark on the beak for the Dyers, two for the Vintners, whilst for those of the Queen, the Seigneur of the Swans, no mark is necessary.

15

Skinners' Hall
Dowgate Hill

The Skinners dealt in skins and fur garments. They were largely wholesalers and retailers of furs, as well as manufacturers of apparel. The actual dressing of skins was performed by a separate craft of tawyers, which later became absorbed into the Skinners' Company.

In the Middle Ages, the wearing of furs was rigidly controlled: only royalty, nobility, and persons of wealth being permitted to adorn themselves in this way.

A residual reminder of this situation, and the use of fur as a mark of distinction being seen in the fur trimming of mayoral and aldermanic robes, and on other ceremonial gowns, and on royal robes and crowns.

Because of the prestige and importance attached to fur, the Company of Skinners attained a prominent place in civic life at an early date, and was among the first of the incorporated Companies of the City, receiving its first charter in 1327.

It shares with the Merchant Taylors, the sixth place in order of precedence amongst the Great Twelve Companies, and is responsible for the governing of Tonbridge School in Kent, which was founded by a former Skinner in the sixteenth century.

The armorial bearings show fur in various forms. Perched aloft is a lynx garlanded with greenery, and below him on either side, are another garlanded lynx, and a marten sable, also wearing a leafy collar, and on the shield are three ermine caps, made in the form of crowns, and a profusion of ermine tails.

An Act of Parliament in the reign of Henry VIII prohibited the wearing of "furres of sables" by any man "under the state of an erle".

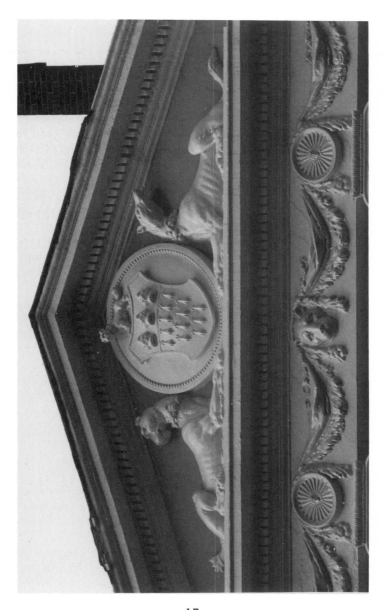

17

The Tallow Chandlers' Hall Dowgate Hill

The Worshipful Company of Tallow Chandlers is the fourteenth Livery Company of the City of London, in order of incorporation.

The records of these early Craft Guilds or 'Misteries', later to become known as Livery Companies, whose reputation for benevolence and hospitality is world wide, are to be found in the wonderful series of memoranda books preserved by the Corporation of London, commencing in the thirteenth century.

It was at this time that the men of different crafts began joining together to foster neighbourly relations, to maintain standards, and to protect themselves against unfair competition.

The Tallow Chandlers were concerned in the main with the manufacture and sale of candles made from animal fat as distinct from bees-wax which was used for church candles, and in the houses of the wealthy.

They supplied the candles that for centuries provided the only means of illumination for the streets of London; the lanthorns in which the candles were placed being made by the Tin Plate Workers and the horn leaves with which these lanthorns were fitted being furnished by the Horners.

The Tallow Chandlers' Company has had a Hall on the same site on Dowgate Hill, leading down to the river, since 1476.

The first Hall was destroyed in the Great Fire of London to be replaced in 1670 mainly by the voluntary contributions of members.

THE BEAVER

Beaver House
Great Trinity Lane

This beaver with his splendidly spatulate rudder-like tail, surmounts the entrance to Beaver Hall, the registered office of the Hudson's Bay Company.

It is in this elaborate neo-Georgian brick building that the great fur sales take place, the Hudson's Bay Company having been incorporated in 1670.

Crouching on a ledge beneath a picture in relief of the "Nonsuch", a vessel which sailed from Gravesend for Hudson Bay in 1668, this beaver appears already to have been trapped for the fur trade.

Quality furs are auctioned by the Hudson's Bay and Annings Ltd. whose sales attract dealers from all over the world, and continue the link with the trappers and hunters who long ago opened up the rich fur areas across the vast newly-explored land of Canada.

NONSUCH

CAPTAIN ZACHARY GILLAM
SAILED FROM GRAVESEND FOR HUDSON BAY
3ʳᵈ JUNE 1668

21

The Worshipful Society of Apothecaries, Blackfriars Lane

The Society of Apothocaries was constituted in 1617 by Royal Charter of James I when the Apothecaries broke away from the Grocers, under whose control the sale of drugs had hitherto been administered. They then became a Craft Guild in their own right. At this time they adopted the rhinoceros for their official crest.

Unicorn horn was one of the most valued of mediaeval drugs, but since the unicorn did not in fact exist, something else had to be used. Originally narwhal horn was an adequate substitute, but with the opening up of Africa, rhinoceros horn was prescribed, and it is still used in Africa as an aphrodisiac. Hence the adoption of the rhinoceros as the crest of the Apothecaries, and its perilous and improbable presence, perched up there upon a coloured wreath.

The Apothecary, who had formerly been concerned with the preparation and sale of drugs for medicinal purposes, in time became the forerunner of the general practitioner.

The Worshipful Society of Apothecaries still remains a livery company, and a licensing body, and it also awards diplomas in The History of Medicine, and The Philosophy of Medicine.

At the turn of the century the pharmaceutical houses took over the manufacture and sale of drugs, and the Society became a purely professional body.

The area in which the Hall stands took its name Blackfriars from the Dominican order which established a Priory there in 1276, and the present buildings were erected after the Great Fire of London.

OPIFERQUE PER ORBEM DICOR

CAMELS COUCHANT

along the Victoria Embankment

Tasselled camels, loaded, and couchant, form both ends of the famous cast-iron seats along the Victoria embankment. The 'arms' are decorated with exotic eastern fruits and flowers, and with fantastic foliage. And the tassels benath the camels' chins, and the ropes that lash the loads to their backs, still show traces of delicately detailed gilding.

The camelled seats charmingly complement the nearby Cleopatra's Needle, a pink granite obelisk erected on the embankment in 1878.

This was an Egyptian obelisk of about 1500 B.C. which has at its base two large bronze sphinxes – creating here in the City of London, a tiny corner of Egypt.

A DRAGON TO MARK
THE ENTRY TO THE CITY

Victoria Embankment
opposite
the Temple Gardens

This fearsome and fabulous monster is a mythical creature usually represented as having the head, wings, and claws of an eagle, and the body and hinder parts of a lion, and is often to be found marking points of entry into the City of London.

Breathing fire and smoke, these dragons occur at various strategic places around the perimeter of the City, drawing attention to its boundaries, and to the risks attendant upon venturing into an area where even the monarch may not enter, except by permission of the Lord Mayor himself.

The origins of this creature probably lie in the ancient east, where, along with other imaginary beasts it is said to have guarded the gold of India.

The Greeks also believed that dragons acted as guardians of the gold mines of the Scythians.

Dragons crop up pretty frequently in heraldry, where they symbolize the combined qualities of two royal creatures. The eagle representing watchfulness, and the lion courage. But to Christians, a dragon signified the dual nature of Christ: the bird part being divine, and the animal standing for the human element.

At any rate, wherever the dragon confronts you with his fearsome countenance, you will know that you are about to enter into its great City.

THE LAMB AND FLAG

Middle Temple
Lincoln's Inn

This was a favourite inn sign in mediaeval times, along the pilgrim routes in Britain, and throughout western Europe.

It represents the Lamb of God, though the origins of this emblem are unclear.

But the inns along the pilgrimage routes of old were reckoned to be recommended, and so to speak given the 'seal of approval' when symbolised by the Lamb and Flag.

The Inns of Court are to-day still linked with those ancient inns.

THE DOG WHO SERVES HIS MASTER
Temple Church

The Temple Church of St. Mary is not a parish church. It is, like Westminster Abbey, a Royal Peculiar.

The nave is circular in the tradition of the Templars, and was consecrated in 1185, and contains some famous marble effigies of thirteenth century Knights.

William Marshall, Second Earl of Pembroke, who died in 1231, rests his feet upon his dog, who has for all those long years remained faithful unto death.

It is often said that the crossed legs are an indication that the deceased had in his lifetime, been to a crusade. And that the exact point where one leg crosses the other, denotes the number of crusades in which this particular Knight took part.

But many people prefer to think that the Knights just look more comfortable and at rest in this position; or that the legs, like the arms – which are so often folded across the breast in death – are perhaps making the sign of the cross.

A snake is coiled upon the Purbeck marble effigy of Heraculus at the east end, south side of the church.

And if you look carefully along the curved walls in 'The Round' where lie the Knights, you will find a monkey, and a sort of giant bat, biting the ears of souls in torment.

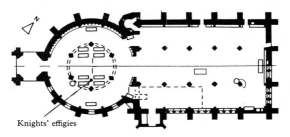

Knights' effigies

A DRAGON

at Bar Gate, Temple Bar
Fleet Street

A gateway of one kind or another, marking the entrance to the City, is thought to have stood on this spot as early as the twelfth century.

The heads of executed traitors and felons were exposed for public viewing on spikes at the top, and Titus Oates in 1685, and Daniel Defoe in 1703, were among many who stood in pillory here.

Since the reign of Elizabeth I, the monarch may not enter the City on State occasions without asking permission to pass Temple Bar. Here, the Sovereign meets the Lord Mayor of London, who surrenders the Sword of State, which is then immediately restored to him, and is carried before the monarch as a symbol of his responsibility for his or her care and protection during this visit to the City.

In the days when there was an actual gate here, it was formally closed on the approach of the Sovereign, and it was required of the herald that he knock thrice upon it, before it was opened.

This little ceremony is said to date from 1588, when Queen Elizabeth I went to St. Paul's Cathedral to give thanks to God for the defeat of the Spanish Armada.

SIGN OF THE THREE SQUIRRELS

19 Fleet Street

There are three squirrels not only on the sign, but also in the upper part of the centre window. These are of lead, and are reputed to be as old as the shield which now hangs just inside the bank building, which dates from early in the seventeenth century.

There is an entry in Pepys' diary dated 1st December 1660, where he records "calling on Mr Pinkney the goldsmith, he took us to the tavern and gave us a pint of wine". This Mr. Pinkney was the original banker of this firm, whose premises in common with much of London, were destroyed in what a contemporary document calls, "the late dismall fire".

The business however continued, and with succeeding partners its nature changed more and more into that of a bank. This is clear from the earliest ledger, still in the bank's possession, dated 1714, which differs little from those in use in the present century.

This bank, Gosling's branch, now forms part of Barclay's Bank, and has been providing banking facilities at this address since 1650.

The goldsmiths who already possessed well-protected strong-rooms, were willing (on agreed terms), to accept desposits of money for safe keeping, issuing receipts for such deposited money. This made trading safer, easier, and less cumbersome; and those receipts given in exchange for money deposited for safe-keeping became the first bank notes.

If you are nuts about squirrels – then there is another one perched on top of a clock at the National Provident Institute building, Eastcheap.

A DOVE AND SERPENT

Serjeants Inn Gates, 49 Fleet Street

These two creatures form part of the coat of arms of the Norwich Union Life Insurance Society.

The coat of arms shows an hour glass with wings, which represents the passage of time, and how time flies by . . . and of the wisdom therefore of making prudent provision for the future with the Society.

The Amicable Society is portrayed by the clasped hands, and the ancient emblem of eternity the serpent, by which they are encircled, gives one to understand and hope that this Friendly Union will endure forever.

But here on the gate we simply have the peaceful dove, and the eternal serpent.

ELEPHANTS

Cutlers' Hall
Warwick Lane

The Cutlers' Company received the first of several Charters in 1416, the year after the Battle of Agincourt. Henry V thereby approved the petition of the "poor people of the Craft of Cutlers within the City of London", for a Grant of Incorporation. The word cutler is derived from the Latin *cultellarius*, as does the old French word *coutelier* (*coutel* meaning a knife), and signifies a maker or seller of knives or other cutting instruments.

The bladers, bladesmiths, or knifesmiths made the blades; the hafters made the hafts or handles; the sheathers made the sheaths; and the cutlers were the skilled men who assembled the various parts, and completed the article. The final touches were given to it by the practised Grinders and Furbishers, who were also concerned with the manufacture of cutlery.

The elephant and castle were granted to the Company as its crest in 1622, the elephant representing the ivory employed in the work of hafting and embellishing the swords, knives, and other weapons.

During the time of the great trade carried on by the East India Company, ivory was unloaded and stored in the vast Ivory Store Houses of St. Katharine's Dock, a practice which has been discontinued now that it is illegal to import ivory into this country.

LION COUCHANT

Monument to Admiral Earl Howe
St. Paul's Cathedral

It is comparatively easy to bag a few lions in the square-mile of the City of London: and lion-hunting can be very productive. Lions as symbols of power, might, and majesty abound: but there's not really too much sport in lion-hunting, there are just too many of them about . . . rampant, couchant, passant, regardant, reargardant . . . any combination of all of these.

They tend to inhabit lofty, inaccessible, conspicuous places, and to look down on everybody, surveying the London scene disdainfully with teeth and claws ominously exposed.

But this is an amiable lion, easy to reach and stroke, with a gentle, mournful expression, submissive and subdued as befits his position at the feet of Admiral Earl Howe, dead since 1799.

Paternoster Square
by St. Paul's Cathedral

Paternoster means 'Our Father', and this statue of the Good Shepherd with his sheep, is by Elisabeth Frink.

It was commissioned by Paternoster Development Ltd, and was unveiled by Yehudi Menuhin on July 30th, 1975.

Bank of England, New Change Watling Street

This building dates from 1953, and houses the Registrar's Department of the Bank of England in Threadneedle Street.

Goldsmiths' Hall
Foster Lane, Cheapside

Goldsmiths' Hall was built between 1829 and 1835, by Philip Hardwick. It is a substantial pleasantly proportioned building of Portland Stone, emerging from the neo-classical style of the early nineteenth century, into a kind of English Baroque.

With giant columns by its entrance and equally massive pilasters on the sides, it has about it much ornamental carving most of it purely representational and elegant, but not specifically to do with gold itself.

But (for our purposes), a fine pair of snakes are flanked by cornucopiae, and a horse with a reptilian tail is surrounded by flags.

A Goldsmiths' Hall has existed on this site since the reign of Edward III (1327–1377). Another building was constructed following damage during the Great Fire in 1666. The remaining structure was demolished in the early 1830's, and the present Hall designed by Philip Hardwick was completed in 1835.

Though the Hall remained virtually unchanged for over a hundred years after that and survived World War I without damage, it narrowly escaped complete destruction in 1941 when the south west wing received a direct hit.

Now, once again it has been lovingly and faithfully restored, and the new repairs are so skilfully carried out that it would be hard for a passer-by to notice them.

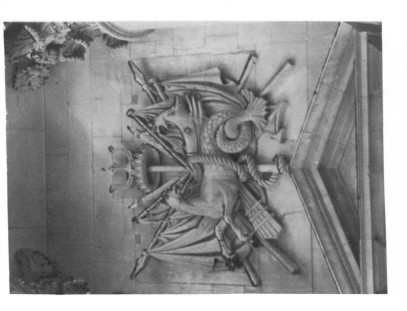

39

Gresham Street, The Worshipful Company of Wax Chandlers

The business of the wax chandlers was the preparation and sale of bees-wax and wax products – mainly candles, from which trade 'chandlers' got its name. Tapers, torches and wax images were also made, and the wax supplied for use as official seals on documents.

In the early days beeswax candles, which were a quality article compared with tallow, were used extensively by the court and nobility, and – prior to the Reformation – by the Church. But the beeswax candles were a luxury up-market product which was only a steady seller to those who could afford such refinements.

At first they were made by the servants for homes, and by the monks for their churches, and it is not until 1298 that a wax chandler is mentioned as supplying wax candles for the less prestigious business of lighting London's streets.

For many years the Worshipful Company of Wax Chandlers flourished: but in time it began to lose control of the trade. By the end of the eighteenth century the introduction of cheaper materials led to the virtual disappearance of beeswax candles.

The Wax Chandlers' Company has kept up the traditions of ceremony, hospitality, and charity during the twentieth century, and it has established links with bee-keeping associations, and with educational institutions. It has also guaranteed in perpetuity, to supply candles for the high altar at St. Paul's.

THE MINOTAUR

Postman's Park
St. Martin's Le Grand

Postman's Park, so called because post office workers from the large G.P.O. nearby could go there to relax, was created from the churchyards of St. Leonard's Foster Lane (which was destroyed and not rebuilt after the Great Fire of 1666), St. Botolph's Aldersgate, and the graveyard of Christ Church Greyfriars, and was laid out as a public garden in 1880.

In 1887 the Victorian artist George Frederick Watts decided that Britain ought to create a national memorial to record for all time, the heroism of a number of men, women, and children who lost their lives as they attempted to save the lives of others.

An actual memorial as such, was never built. But in the course of time, an open gallery was constructed in Postman's Park, and a number of individual tablets were placed there, to commemorate the various touching acts of unselfish bravery by which lives were given by young and old. Brave deeds performed by heroes in humble walks of life.

The statue of the Minotaur by the modern British Sculptor, Michael Ayrton, dominates the eastern end of the park. A monster from Greek mythology, with a bull's head, and a human body, for which Daedalus built the Labyrinth, is here portrayed as a creature of immense power and strength.

The Minotaur was set up to mark the spot where a public house called The Bull and Mouth used to stand.

HERBERT MACONOCHU
SCHOOL BOY FROM WIMBLEDON AGED 13
HIS PARENTS ABSENT IN INDIA. LOST
HIS LIFE IN VAINLY TRYING TO RESCUE
HIS TWO SCHOOL FELLOWS WHO WERE
DROWNED AT GLOVERS POOL CROYDE.
NORTH DEVON • AUGUST 28 1882.

HERBERT PETER CAZALY
STATIONER'S CLERK
WHO WAS DROWNED AT KEW
IN ENDEAVOURING TO SAVE
A MAN FROM DROWNING
APRIL 21 1889

JAMES HEWERS
ON SEPT 24 1878
WAS KILLED BY A TRAIN
AT RICHMOND IN THE
ENDEAVOUR TO SAVE
ANOTHER MAN.

HARRY SISLEY OF
KILBURN AGED 10
DROWNED IN ATTEMPTING
TO SAVE HIS BROTHER
AFTER HE HIMSELF HAD
JUST BEEN RESCUED
MAY 24 1878

The Worshipful Company of Ironmongers
Ironmongers' Hall, The Barbican

The Ironmongers, originally known as the Ferroners (the French word for iron is *fer*), were established as a craft and fellowship in the thirteenth century. They are one of the Twelve Great Livery Companies of the City of London.

They purchased their first Hall in Fenchurch Street in 1457, and received their first charter of incorporation in 1463.

The Company's third Hall, built in 1750, was one of the few buildings in London to be bombed in the First World War.

The present Hall was completed on a new site in Aldersgate Street in 1925. The Company was spared the devastation of the Great Fire in 1666, and suffered only limited damage in World War II.

As a result, many of the Company's early records are still in its possession. The Court books are complete from 1555, as is the list of freemen since that date, and the names of nearly all its Masters since its founding, are known.

The salamanders which support the shield on the Company's crest are mythological reptiles, a sort of tailed amphibian somewhat resembling a lizard, and with a soft moist skin, reputed to be fire-proof, and said to live in fire.

A very suitable creature to be connected with the blacksmith's trade, and the heating of coal or charcoal, with glowing fires, and red hot embers.

45

Guildhall
Guildhall Yard

The Guildhall has been used as a meeting place, and before there were Law Courts, as a Law Court. Here the elected representatives have always met to plan and organise City business, as those who represent the City's Wards still do to-day.

But the Guildhall itself, dating back to 1411 has suffered grieviously from fires and from bombs. It is the most important of all the Halls erected by the Guilds in the Middle Ages, and here, as a Law Court, sentence of death was passed on the Earl of Surrey, on Cranmer, on Lady Jane Grey, and others.

After the Lord Mayor's Show, the new Lord Mayor holds his first official Dinner and Reception in this Hall: a banquet at which the guest of honour is always the Prime Minister.

The Guildhall, London, dating from the mediaeval period, had a Gothic-like façade (1789), the work of George Dance the younger. Later, in 1864 a handsome roof designed by the City architect Sir Horace Jones altered the appearance of the building, which had already been restored by Sir Christopher Wren after the havoc wrought by the Great Fire of 1666.

But the Guildhall was to be damaged yet again, and on the night of December 29th, 1940, when the neighbouring church of St. Lawrence Jewry was reduced to a smouldering shell, the roof of the Guildhall too was destroyed as the 'blitz' on London's City ravaged 'the square mile'.

47

St. Lawrence Jewry
next Guildhall

After the Great Fire of London had virtually destroyed St. Lawrence Jewry, the church was rebuilt by Sir Christopher Wren, and was reopened for worship in 1677.

At this time, in keeping with the Wren tradition, the windows were of white glass set in lead, and were supported by saddle bars which conformed to the shape of the arched openings into which they fitted.

During the latter half of the last century, this plain glass was replaced by coloured glass depicting Bible stories, and giving a warm glow, whilst at the same time permitting sufficient daylight to enter the church. But all these windows were destroyed when the church was burned out by enemy action during the night of December 29th, 1940.

The St. George window is centrally placed in the north wall, and on either side are windows containing the arms and emblems of the Sovereign Independent States of the Commonwealth in 1957: the year of the restoration of this, the official church of the Corporation of the City of London.

The Lord Mayor's pew is in front on the right, and is flanked by those of the Queen's Sheriffs. There are pews too for the Aldermen, and in the south aisle, for the Esquires.

The City's Coat of Arms is on the organ gallery; its flag is on the south sanctuary wall; and in front of the Lord Mayor's pew is the Swordrest, and the table for the Mace to rest on during the service. Five civic services are attended here in state each year.

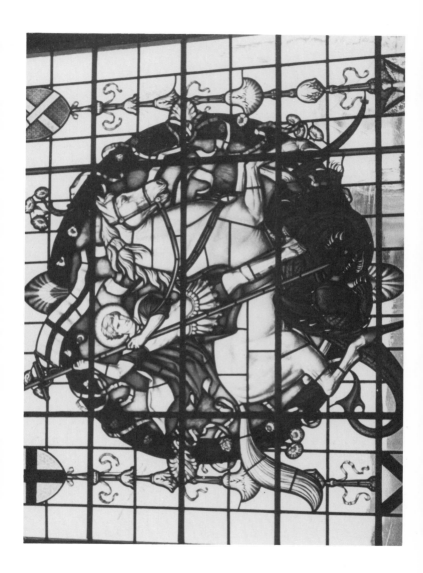

Grocers' Hall
Prince's Street

Tucked away to the west of Prince's Street is the Grocers' Company. Dating from 1345 when it was founded by 22 Pepperers, and known at that time as the Fraternity of St. Antony, they did not in fact obtain a charter until 1428. They were appointed inspectors of such merchandise as spices, drugs, herbs, etc., though at that time they did not call themselves Grocers. In those days Grocers also dealt in whale-oil, wool, and cotton; and in 1607 they were incorporated with the Apothecaries though this union was dissolved in 1615.

The present imposing Hall was built in 1893, but was badly damaged by fire in 1965, and required extensive rebuilding.

A camel and nine cloves adorn the Grocers' Coat of Arms: a reminder of their association over many years with the trade in fragrant products imported from the near and far east.

Antony the Great, A.D. 251–356, was a Christian saint and hermit who distributed his property among the poor,

GOD GRANT GRACE

and retired to the Egyptian desert to live his life in solitude.

He is usually depicted as an old man who wears a beard and a monk's cloak, and leans upon a T-shaped stick. He holds a bell, and is always accompanied by a pig. The Antonine monks in the Midde Ages kept and bred pigs whose lard was said to have been used as a remedy for St. Anthony's Fire.

The bell is sometimes shown as hanging around the pig's neck, and in the seventeenth century the pigs belonging to the Hospital Brothers of St. Antony were allowed special grazing rights, and were therefore distinguished in this way.

THE GRASSHOPPER
Lombard Street

In the days of Queen Elizabeth I, the princely merchant and goldsmith Sir Thomas Gresham, who did much for posterity in founding the Royal Exchange, and Gresham College, had his shop called The Grasshopper on this site.

The family crest of the Greshams was the grasshopper, and it is supposed that he named his shop after this little creature.

Later on, between 1637 and 1665, a goldsmith by the name of Clement Punge lived here, and in 1677 Messrs. Dunscombe and Kent continued the business of goldsmithery from these premises.

It is possible to trace a whole series of goldsmiths who had their place of business here.

To-day the grasshopper still adorns the school tie of a Gresham College boy; and Lombard Street continues to be full of banks and bankers, whose pioneering forbears were the Goldsmiths of old, with their safe deposits, and their impenetrable vaults.

This, number 68 Lombard Street was once Martin's Bank, but now forms part of Barclay's network of banking premises.

THE CAT-A-FIDDLING

Lombard Street

This sign on the west corner of Birchin Lane, in Lombard Street, used to be called The Cat-a-Fiddling, and a very unusual sign it was too, because in most other places where it occurs, it is usually called The Cat and Fiddle.

In 1672, and possibly even a little earlier, it was the sign of Anthony Dansie, a haberdasher, who built this house, and who died in 1677.

In 1654–5, he and other merchants petitioned for, and were granted permission by the Lord Protector, to export to Barbados 900 dozen pairs of boots, and five tons of cheese.

His widow, Mary, who died in 1717 at Romford, left her property to her grandchildren. And later in 1779, James Upjohn, a watchmaker, carried on his business from these premises.

54

A DOG'S HEAD

on Aldegate Pump
Aldgate

'Aldegate' well, adjoining the City wall, existed here in the time of King John – 1199–1216.

Later, towards the end of the sixteenth century, a pump was erected over the well. In earlier times, since the well had been connected with a chapel which had existed close by, medicinal and holy virtues were claimed for the water.

But chemical tests on the water later on, found it to be dangerous to the health of the people, and in 1876 the well was filled in, and a cistern below ground level, and connected with the New River supply, was put in its place.

But Aldegate pump still stands, enclosed in ornamental stone casing, its spout of bronze in the shape of a dog's head being, over so many years, polished almost clean away.

All-Hallows-By-The-Tower
Byward Street

As Founder Padre of Talbot House TOC H. Poperinghe, in 1915, the Rev. 'Tubby Clayton' created a home from home for Allied soldiers, which became for many a source of physical and spiritual recreation.

Called Talbot House in memory of Lt. Gilbert Talbot, killed at Ypres, troops referred to Talbot House by its initials, in 'telegraphese', as TOC H.

Philip Thomas Byard Clayton, CH, MC, DD, FSA, 1885–1972, became vicar of All-Hallows in 1922, and remained there until 1963.

He had several small Scottish terriers over the years, all of them call 'Chippy', and all of them given to him by the Queen Mother, from Windsor.